Even If...

Written by Judy Billing
Illustrated by Olha Tkachenko

Dedicated to four precious little boys, who grew up to be four wonderful men.

To my sons – Jeff, Brad, Derrick and Kevin.

With love from Mom!

EVEN IF...
Billing, Judy - author, 2018
Illustrations, layout & design by Olha Tkachenko, Little Big Me Publishing, 2018
WWW.LITTLEBIG.ME
All rights © Judy Billing. No part of this publication may be reproduced, stored in retrieval system, or transmitted in any form or by any means: electronic, mechanical, photocopying, recording, or otherwise, without the prior written permission of the author.

1 Thessalonians 5:18

Give thanks in all circumstances, for this is God's will for you in Christ Jesus.

It's fun to say thanks for a sun-shiny day,
When our friends come to call and they want us to play.
When Mom gives permission to take out our toys,
We go play outside with the girls and the boys.

We're feeling quite fine and we're happy today.
Things are tickety-boo and we like it this way!
It's good to say thank you to God up above.
It's a wonderful day and we're feeling His love!

But when kids treat us mean and they poke and they pry,
They make us feel bad and we just want to cry.
Then we sit all alone while they run and they play.
We're feeling quite sad. We're not happy today.

Even if this should happen; even if this comes true,
We'll still thank You, Jesus, for all that You do.
For all that You are, Your praises we'll sing.
You still wear the Crown and You still are the King!

When Mom's baking cookies,
she offers us one.
Sometimes we can help and
we join in the fun!
When Dad takes us fishing
and we hold the rod,
At the end of the day, it's fun
to thank God.

We like to go camping on a warm summer night.
We sleep under the stars and we watch them shine bright.
We eat marshmallows toasted, all gooey and sweet.
We say thank you to Jesus for this wonderful treat!

But when the sky fills with clouds and the rain's pouring down,
We have nothing to do and no friends around,
Our sister's a pest, she won't leave us alone,
This seems a good day to moan and to groan.

Even if this should happen; even if this comes true,
We'll still thank You, Jesus, for all that You do.
For all that You are, Your praises we'll sing.
You still wear the Crown and You still are the King!

We're off to see Grandma. How fun it will be!
She's sure to have treats and she loves to see me!
She'll hug me and tell me that I am the best.
It's fun to say thanks when I'm feeling blessed!

She'll read us a story and we'll go for a walk.
She'll sit down and listen if we want to talk.
She'll show us old photos and make us a snack.
We'll say thank you to Jesus. We want to go back!

But if I fall off my bike and I hurt my knee,
And I have an ouchie, I think you'll agree,
I'm not very happy when I'm feeling pain,
It's hard to say thank you to Jesus again.

Even if this should happen; even if this comes true,
We'll still thank You, Jesus, for all that You do.
For all that You are, Your praises we'll sing.
You still wear the Crown and You still are the King!

There's a circus in town and Dad says we'll go.
How fun! How exciting! It'll be a great show!
There'll be lions and tigers and elephants to boot,
And seals that blow horns with a tootley-toot!

We've had a great time with the family today.
When we go to bed, it'll be easy to pray
A big thank you to Jesus, a hip hip hooray!
We feel loved and happy.
It's been a good day!

But if we're wearing new shoes and our toes start to hurt,
If we trip and we stumble and fall in the dirt,
If we stop to smell flowers, so pretty to see,
And we feel a sharp sting on our nose – OUCH! A bee!

Even if this should happen; even if this comes true,
We'll still thank You, Jesus, for all that You do.
For all that You are, Your praises we'll sing.
You still wear the Crown and You still are the King!

At the end of each day, the good and the bad,
Jesus wants us to thank Him for all that we've had.

No matter how lovely, no matter if not,
For things we remember and things we forgot.

He's always beside us, with you and with me.
There's nothing can touch us, I know you'll agree,

Unless He allows it, for He is the King.
So we ALWAYS thank Jesus. His praises we'll sing!!

www.ingramcontent.com/pod-product-compliance
Lightning Source LLC
Chambersburg PA
CBHW061121170426
43209CB00013B/1628